Door
to
Door

Praise for Emma Walton Hamilton

"I don't just want to read poems like this, I want to read essays about poems like this, I want to see the cinema, the photography, the paintings that poems like this could inspire... Remarkable!" —**Raymond Antrobus,** poet, 2021 Bridport International Poetry Prize judge

"Emma Walton Hamilton's *Door to Doo*r contains an exuberant range of poetic forms and structures and with it her willingness to try just about anything." —**Billy Collins,** U.S. Poet Laureate

"Walton Hamilton wears her yoke lightly, her poems immersed and persistently optimistic about the constraints of familiarity... But even into the deepest crevasse 'drops a seed / of hope,' and out of the rift comes poetry." —**Julie Sheehan,** Whiting Award–winning poet

DOOR
TO
DOOR

POEMS

EMMA WALTON HAMILTON

Andrews McMeel
PUBLISHING®

For Steve, Sam, and Hope,
who supported me on every step of this journey
with patience, encouragement, and love.

CONTENTS

HOMELAND

Bowmont Drive

A slick vinyl banquette,
butter-yellow, circling a white Formica table.

A semi-circular driveway,
each end reaching down to the road,
like a frowny face with window eyes
and a door-shaped nose.

In the back, a small pond set in brick;
Japanese carp drift near the surface,
flashing pink and white before disappearing
into the inky depths.

Banquette, driveway, pond.
Three circles.
Nuclei of my beginnings.

Joint Custody

The red carpet of the terminal passage
holds no glamour.
Six times a year, I embark or disembark
through this birth canal

                                     UP towards departures

or DOWN towards arrivals,
my emotions turbulent each way.

The concrete arms designed to embrace the traveler
can't offer what I need.
Curved white walls undulate

                                        up and down

in and away
as I journey

                                          East

or West
clutching Dad's Witch Hazel–scented handkerchief
                       or Mom's repurposed pocketbook

                  to ground me
              as I reinvent myself
                 again.

Door to Door

William Arthur Morris had a birthmark in the center of his back.
Wrong side of the sheets, they said
and banished him to the scullery.
He volunteered for the army
and took a post as camp barber.

William Arthur Morris deserted the Guards
five days after the birth of his daughter.
Bad character, said the discharge papers.
Fifteen shillings and twenty-nine days
for his cardinal sin.

William Arthur Morris upped sticks to a pit village.
Deputy Artist, they called him
at smoking concerts. Two up, two down, with a privy and coal
while his wife scrubbed soot from their sheets
in Temperance Street.

William Arthur Morris sold poems door to door.
He tickled the fancies of toffs and swells,
until he went to the Sanitorium, with the pox he contracted
from his entertainments.
Paralysis of the insane, said my great-grandfather's death papers.

Over the Tannoy

(A conversation with my great-grandfather, William Arthur Morris, "The Pitman's Poet." Arthur's words are in the left column, mine are on the right.)

I wish	*I could read your Poems*
to inform the public	*not just the horses*
that several men	*the ones I don't know*
have been duplicating	*your active workings... so*
my Poems and	*I could own them. It would be like you and I*
are going door to door	*or maybe like I am unearthing your bones*
selling Pirate copies	*as if they were mine, every one*
of them.	
On the 9th March 1922,	*decades ago*
a Warrant was issued	*between our lifetimes*
for the arrest of a man who	*sounds crazy I know but*
had traveled	*in a shaft of light*
through Yorkshire,	*quite a bit farther than*
Notts and Derbyshire and	*anywhere, you*
sold thousands of copies	*and I fused at the core*
of my Poem.	
He also stated in some cases	*beyond genetics*
that he was authorized	*mystically or cosmically*
by me to sell them.	*you might say*
This is entirely a falsehood,	*it's undeniable*
as I employ NO agents.	*I am, like you, drilling*
All my Poems are	*in a similar vein, sometimes*
Copyright and fully protected	*to a fault*
and are entirely my own	*but these days that*
composition and property	*isn't enough, it must be a Poem*
and every one has	*to be mined as if it were*
my own Photograph	*revealing your bones*
(as above)	*there's that thread again*
on the front	*on the face*
of it.	*a fissure in everything I write*

Should an imposter call
and offer any of my Poems
for sale,
will you kindly inform
the Police
and oblige.

I will read your words
not to assess their value
but to fathom my own, and
the Muse
or anyone else who might answer

The Accident of Birth

The orchid in the wood blooms, providential
Illumined by a single shaft of light
Predestined to achieve its full potential
Protected from impediment or blight.

The dandelion in the field must labor
Withstanding any unforgiving gale
Struggling for resource without favor
Enduring tribulation and travail.

The traveler who lunches in the shade
Remarks upon the orchid's splendid hue
Imagines it upon lapel displayed
And plucks it from the peat moss where it grew.

In the field, the dandelion's face
Turns to the sun, appreciative of grace.

Chemistry

You smell like toast
You leave your socks on
You jeté across the oatmeal carpet
You lasso flies with strands of hair
You like to watch
You sleep under your pillow
You suck your harmonica with eyes closed
In cooking, you're a porn star
In loving, a flying Wallenda
You make my bread rise.

Social Litany
(after Billy Collins)

I am a Golden Retriever,
a Cockatiel, and a Sloth Bear.
I am also Shortbread,
an Ocean Swimmer, and
a Saucy Snuggler.

I belong in Edwardian England.

You are probably a Great Dane,
an Emperor Penguin, and a Panda.
No doubt you are also Oatmeal Raisin,
a Muse Worshipper,
and a Lusty Lip Locker.

Bohemian Paris is where you belong.

These things are unreliable, of course.
It was two years earlier When I Lost My Virginity,
and I'm certainly not a Shetland Pony.

But I am *definitely* English Breakfast Tea.

You, on the other hand,
are undeniably a Palomino
and—I'm guessing—a Double Espresso.

How I long to be a Palomino.

At least we have one thing in common.
Neither of us are the boots in the corner.

The Tuning Fork in the Bathroom

Head erect and tines astride,
the armless conductor invites the chamber
to resonate with acoustic assonance.

But there are no strings in this ensemble,
no ebony or brass. Only porcelain and tile,
glass and chrome.

Where has it come from? Who stationed it here?
And what is the value of sine waves at the fundamental frequency
in this miniature suite?

I relocate this pitch-fork, but it invariably returns
to its post between the his-and-hers sinks,
harmonizing with each brush and flush, and humming

while I fiddle with my hair, pick or pluck
at minor divertissements, and compose myself
in prelude to the day.

Sonata

In Hirschfeld's striking portrait of Bernstein,
the maestro poises, baton raised.

Will the downbeat begin the concerto?
Or is it a rest, as his brow suggests,
strained with the agony—or ecstasy—
of the symphony inside his head?

Chin up, mouth set, hands larger than life
like the man himself,
he is all head and shoulders
just as he stood above the rest.

A hint of Nina lines his unkempt hair
in Hirschfeld's striking portrait of Bernstein.

Lexington Avenue

have you seen the stork?
we deliver
       god bless you mami
             hey baby   fresh catch
                  oyster of the day   get your sweat on
                      we're open
what's up beautiful?
have a good day
       zen palace
             psychic readings   please
                 pardon our appearance   we're open
                   no ball playing
hey what's up girl?
barista wanted
       send a salami
             we buy gold   park here
                damn, girl
                      we're open
     no cuts and colors
         just blowouts
            please
            excuse the inconvenience   everything
                 must go   wrong way

we're open baby slow down   coming soon
hey   hey   hey   hey
     do not cross   do not park   do not overload
       now streaming
          park   park here   park here now
               enter
                  enter
                     enter
                        enter

STOP.

Homeland
(after Gerard Manley Hopkins)

Praise be to bounteous British sludge—
  Slathering Wellies with each squelch and suck;
    For slop, teeming with life in tell-tale squirts;
Mineral-rich worm casts, dense as fudge;
  Landscape trod and puddled—wallow, clart, and muck;
    And every form of stabble, retch, and dirt.

Sediment, sluther, slurry, and slick;
  A kingdom of glorious gloppy guck,
    From whence came whattle-and-daub, wychert,
Clay, stoneware, porcelain, and brick.

Narcissae

The bulbs of my subconscious
beneath the snow of ignorance
and topsoil of distraction
reproduce and multiply,
until, invasive now,
they manifest.

I must dig, divide and redistribute;
cultivate more daffodils,
and fewer chives.

RELOCATION

Relocation

Today's walk on the beach
yields a cluster of treasures,
each its own biosphere.

A Moon Snail, accommodating someone else's eggs.
A family of Slipper Snails, clinging to a Scallop.
A Quahog Clam, teeming with seawater and sand. A micro-ocean.

The host shells are otherwise empty,
neither landlord nor tenants having anticipated the tide
or the inevitable seagull.

I played God for a moment,
placing each one gently back in the surf—
cleaving to hope.

Redwood Road

Buddha in his Yankees cap beams under the river birch,
as oblivious to the deer-lopped lilies and beheaded pansies
as he was to the mountain of snow just weeks ago.

Across the road, a pair of ospreys circle the radio tower,
whistling warnings to onlookers and passersby
while their new nest vibrates with Golden Oldies.

Whodunit

"Applebee's Alligator"
might be the title of a children's book
in which the toothy hero dons an apron
and discovers his calling:
serving up
good food for good people,
carside-to-go.

But the character who parked his pet
by the Mastic-Shirley Applebee's, in a small plastic tub
with "My Gator" scrawled along the side,
probably had a different story in mind.

Maybe his take-out double-crunch shrimp
had just become finger food.

Or was it the perfect alibi
he saw posted in Applebee's window, proclaiming:
"SHIRLEY. Long Island's Best Kept Secret"?

Sunday Breakfast

Hers are first.
Silver dollar–sized, with just a touch
of light amber, ordered by the gallon
from Dad's ancestral home.

Mine are next.
Plain brown. Egg on one,
strips either side. No berries, please.
Don't mix Mom's sweet and salty.

Time for manly acrobatics.
How large can still be flipped?
Two Handyman Specials, plate-sized,
pushing every boundary
but for the vegan sausage.

A Venn diagram
of family relations.

On the Eve of my Son's Sixteenth Birthday

Sixteen.

   I exist!

      Seen six,
          ten.

            Teens? Tense.
            (Sex. Sin. Text. Ex.)

Next?

          Set tie.

               Exit nest.

Childishness
(after Frank O'Hara)

When I was a child
I hung with the grown-ups,
desperate to be
one of them.

I never babysat,
had no dolls,
and avoided anyone
younger than myself.

In 6th grade I wore eye shadow
applied (and then removed) on the bus
and high heels at all times,
even on the cobblestones.

Now here I am,
with children
the center of my life...
a geode, cracked open,
sparkling!

High Hopes

Despite susceptibility to stress
—aphid, canker, beetle, blight, or gale—
your rosy face and valor still impress
and, toughened by each hardship, you prevail.

Like you, she has her challenges to face.
You've more in common than your fitting name.
She copes with wit, ferocity, and grace;
your radiant strength of spirit is the same.

Yet you, with lanky stem bowed by your height
—a too-tall lady, slouching in her stance—
now nod toward the wind and, with delight,
accept his invitation to the dance.

Oh, let her your resilience acquire.
For hope you give, and Hope you may inspire.

The News

The spacecraft lands on a comet
that roars like a Hollywood alien
and smells of rotten eggs and horse urine.

Charles Manson is engaged to marry his twenty-something fiancée
and a Pastafarian wears a colander on her head
for her driver's license photo.

If you buy a pink house in Florida,
you may find a corpse in the master bedroom.

Global Warming

The burst spigot sprays the river birch
with upside down rain,
sheathing every branch in frozen glass.

A hundred slender jewel cases,
refracting winter light
and magnifying the showpiece within.

One by one, the casings drop
to the pock-marked snow beneath,
fractured vials littering the walkway

leaving hung-over branches
to droop and drip, in memory
of crystal-induced radiance.

Maybe Tomorrow

Twenty-seven pairs of earrings dangle and invite;
She wears the small gold hoops.

A dozen chains and chokers adorn the mirror;
She wears the hammered gold peace sign.

Rings and bracelets cluster in assorted jewelry boxes.
She wears a serviceable silver watch,
and four rings—engagement, wedding, anniversary
and grandmother's.

The make-up bag is full of options:
concealer, eyeliner, lipstick, blush,
a rainbow of eye shadows.
She simply wears mascara.

Candy-colored nail polish in baskets
is used only by her daughter.
Her nails are short, the polish clear.

Her closet is stuffed with sweaters,
slacks, skirts, jackets, and dresses.
She reaches again for jeans
and a black T-shirt.

Day after day, night after night
she turns to these faithful friends.
They are as much a part of her body as her skin and hair.

Maybe tomorrow she'll break out her stilettos
or ride a unicycle down Main Street
topless.

Today, she picks up the children,
the marriage, the day's work,
      and her familiars,
and wraps them around her
for cover.

The Beauty of Anne Carson

I loathe this man
this husband
who boasts of his mistress with shy pride
and only feels clean when he wakes
with his wife.

Who likes folly and bruises
writes pretentious poems with no return address
and lies about money, meetings,
and his origins.
Who cannot be trusted by a mother
or a grandfather
let alone a wife.

Why does this woman
this wife
who writes ecstatic, unknowable, cutthroat, glad
tangos with language and holds beauty
say Beauty is Truth
and waste her maidenhood, her words,
her breath
on this bastard?

To shut the box
because her wounds give off light.

Revision

I peel the poem like an orange,
revealing all the flesh and juice beneath.

Or maybe it's an onion, with each layer
becoming more translucent and refined.

But then, perhaps an artichoke is best,
with every leaf containing its own message.

Preparing me, one nibble at a time,
to find the sweet and salty heart within.

THE SWAMP ANGEL

Poems inspired by the memoir and writings of
author/philosopher Prentice Mulford, 1834–1891.

"... the Swamp Angel broods in his gloom."
—Herman Melville, "The Swamp Angel"

Swamp Angel

Two years of my forty-nine
spent as an indifferent sailor;
twelve in California,
digging a little gold
and a good deal of dirt.

I have taught school, tended bar, kept a grocery,
stacked mail, collected tax, policed men,
sorted seagull eggs, started a hog ranch,
and prospected for silver.

I ran a hotel into the ground,
and a farm to weeds.

I killed a coyote.

I have seen Cape Horn, London, Paris, Vienna,
a whale in a flurry,
and a ship's crew in mutiny.

I have lectured,
and written for the papers.

I have an ex-mother-in-law.

And the world has returned kick for kick,
frown for frown,
smile for smile.

But I have had no adventure,
no success, no failure
as great as in this house I built
in the woods, in a swamp, with a spring nearby,
beside a noble, wide-branching oak.

My faults, whatever they are,
within these four walls
trouble no one but myself.

I can leave my slippers
as I took them off,
one toe pointing north, the other south
and find them a week afterward
in the same position.

I fear not to leave mud on my own carpet.
I am tormented by no neighbors' culinary smells.

I keep hens.

Yet I have hardly touched the edge of life
and know little what it means to live
save
thoughts are things.

Thought Forces

Thoughts run in stream-like currents,
fine rills of life-feeding-life
or injurious poisons
stinging all they touch.

The arrow tipped with ill will
is deadliest to its archer,
and fear and fault attract
more of their currency.

But the open heart invites
positive force, globules
of quicksilver melding
to become one body

which, when sparked,
ignite the power within.

Sufficient unto the Day

A heap of castaways takes refuge
in a corner of my house.
Baskets, a satchel, assorted tin boxes,
a pot lid, bereft of its pot.

An onion joins this disorganized rebellion,
and two potatoes, alternately freezing and thawing.
In the crevices are bits of rope,
string, rags, nails, and tacks.

I endeavor to carry out the law—
but an iron cooking spoon engages me in lively quarrel.
Devoid of occupation or fixed station,
it wanders o'er the house, in a state of vagrancy.

As much useless lumber of fact, opinion, event, date,
resides in my mind—
another badly governed empire
wherein insurrection brews.

The floor needs scrubbing, the teakettle leaks,
a lath is off the hen-coop.
There are letters to write, stovepipes to be jointed,
and bread to be made.

Besides which, I want, of all things,
a rhubarb pie.

And where has that knife gone to?

This mob of wants,
desires, plans, whims, aspirations
captures and enslaves me... each yelling his demand,
and insisting on being served first.

I bring in more things to aid the domestic economy
but the more I do,
the greater the war
and the harder it is to put down the uprising.

Body in the hencoop and mind in the kitchen
results in a bloody finger and a burned corncake.

Questions of Order

Shall I go on putting joint to my stovepipe,
length on length, until it pierces high heaven?

How much of my youthful book-cramming
has provided extra stovepipe knowledge?

Is the mind a magazine, a rag bag, a closet under the stairs
to be filled with odds and ends of information?

Or is it a mirror, to be polished
so that it shall reflect in itself all that is?

And is the polishing process
like the cramming process?

The Commute

Each morning, I foot the mile to the railway station
and reach the city by half past seven.

At the newspaper office, I make a summary
of the same eternal round of events—

Murders, burglaries, suicides
by pistol, razor, rope, or poison,
embezzlements (high-toned),
thefts (low-toned),
smash-ups, fires, burst boilers,
falling elevators, gas explosions,
kerosene burnings, failures,
and everything else

—which happens in all civilized communities
just the same, one year after another,
the only difference being that the victim
or the villain
has a different name this year
from the same date last.

I wonder why people are interested in reading
such a monotonous and ghastly catalogue of horrors
as I dish up for them daily.

I wonder if they will so continue to read
through all eternity, in case their lives are spared
that somewhat incomputable period.

I wonder what the profit is of knowing
after you have eaten your breakfast cakes and sausage
that a tramp was found last night hanging from a tree in Central Park

or that an idiot killed himself with prussic acid and died
on a park bench where possibly you may sit tomorrow,
because the girl he wanted to marry and make miserable
preferred to be married and made miserable
by some other idiot.

Yet I serve up this intellectual stew
made from the ingredients of our barbaric civilization
with a tolerably clear conscience.

First, because I am well paid for it.
Second, because I like the work.
And third, because the public wants their daily horrors
spiced as I spice them.

And then I fly back by rail
to my beloved swamp,
where I labor until dusk
overlooked only by an occasional crow
perched on a neighboring sycamore
cross, tired, and hungry
because there is no young corn yet
to pull up.

Brooding in the Gloom

Despite all I have done to gain seclusion
the cares of the outside world invade;
I parry against every small intrusion,
outwitted by decisions to be made.

Whether to have toast or eggs for breakfast;
buy a hoe or borrow from my neighbor.
Whether to plant cabbages or lettuce;
repair my roof with tin, or tar and paper.

Whether to buy a ten-dollar knapsack
or make a sixty-five cent one suffice.
Whether to scold the absentminded bootblack
for shoddiness of shine, or tip him twice.

Yet in these thousand thoughts of every day,
which I am well ashamed to here confess
—I shall or shall not, should or shouldn't, may—
I am Creator of my own distress.

And while I trudge from swampland home to train,
my thoughts a muddle and my will opaque,
Nature does her best to entertain
with the splendors of a sunrise on the lake.

Omega

After all, the house proved a failure
so far as my contentment was concerned.

When it was finished,
and my corn was coming up,
and my hens were in laying order,
and three had commenced setting,
and the morning glory vines
had commenced peeping in at the front windows,
I commenced to mope.

I had imagined I could live happily, alone with nature
and largely independent of the rest of the human race.

Nature herself has taught me better.

Birds go in pairs and flocks,
plants and trees grow in families,
ants live in colonies,
and everything of its kind has a tendency to live and grow
together.

But here was I,
a single bit of humanity
trying to live alone and away from my kind.

"You don't belong to us," the birds and trees said.
"You belong to your own. Go join them again. Cultivate them."

A hermit is one who tries to be a tree,
and draw nourishment from one spot
when he's really a great deal more.

A bear is not so foolish as to try and live among foxes,
neither should a man try to live among trees
because they can't give him all that he must have
to make the most of life.

So I left my hermitage,
I presume forever,
and carted my bed, and pots and pans
to the house of a friend
perched on the brink
of the palisades opposite Tinker's.

INSIDE OUT

Spring Cleaning

They swarm the house, red-shirted, armed
with weapons of transformation.
Within minutes they infiltrate every room
and begin the attack.

My husband hides out in his shed,
the dog and I take refuge on the sofa; senses bombarded
by the hum of vacuum cleaners
and the stinging smell of carpet shampoo.

Each individual, milestone, and pull-back
has left its mark. The residue of ten thousand meals
clings to the cabinets and surfaces with gummy force.

Time was we managed the melee,
or made peace with creative chaos.
Now we are overwhelmed.

But the cavalry has come at last,
to rescue us from our entrenchment.

Vanity

Hairclips on the gooseneck lamp
tortoiseshell and black

beside a wedding portrait.
Smell of make-up

clumped in bags and jars.
On the mirror,

necklaces, and photos of children
aged by the sun.

His pants
draped over the chair.

Control Alt Escape

Our affiliate status took some customizing.
No need for prospect verification,
your profile triggered my autoresponder immediately.

But campaigns and broadcasts were out of the question,
so I engaged in some persuasive upsell, and eventually
you opted in; no domains masked.

We bounced, soft and hard, through custom fields,
bundling products into recurring orders,
my portal always receptive to your input.

Errors were made along the way...
our defaults needed resetting from time to time, and
we had to blacklist one or two third-party integrations.

But here we are, still linked, still active,
no expiration date in sight.

L.E.M.

The box is small.
The picture black and white.
Grains of snow across an ashy surface.
Someone—the Pillsbury doughboy? The Michelin Man?
—hatches from a crab-like creature and undulates
in slow motion.
Giant steps.

The building is large, empty, and black.
It smells of beer and dust and vomit.
The creature grew here.
We clean, and build, and light
and people stream in
to watch each other and themselves.
Giant steps.

The room is small and windowless.
A desk, a chair, a plastic plant.
Behind the vault-thick door with massive lock
the creature lay in wait.
In the echoing space below,
the creatures of my imagination sing.
Giant steps.

Global Warming, Part II

At what point in this roller coaster of a winter
did the pylons catapult from their beds?

Somewhere between the accelerating wind
and plummeting temperatures,
beneath summits of snow and immeasurable ice,
they broke their banks.

I imagine their thrill in time-lapse mode,
as they defied nature, logic, and gravity,
groaning with every thrust and corkscrew turn,
lurching to dizzying new heights.

They never guessed the ride would be one-way
or that their lack of restraint would leave them exposed,
camel-backed and teetering
on the edge of Paynes Creek.

Inside Out

Inside out
for the count
down to the ground
zero
tolerance for ambiguity
of meaning
of life
is but a dream.

Inside out
of order
of business casual
affairs of the state
of mind made up
to no good.

Inside out
of time to spare
parts of a sentence
commuted between
the sheets of the winds
of change
of heart
of gold rush to judgment days
of plenty
of nothing
gold can stay.

Inside out
of control group
leader
of the pack
of lies
in wait for it
can't happen here

and there
but
for the grace of god
given rights
of passage
of time of your life
is beautiful
inside
and out.

Eruption

The fact that most of the Island is sewer-less was apparently news
to those who escaped to their seaside cottages and mansions,
unaware that septic tanks need to be emptied regularly.

Systems designed to handle a certain amount of flow
per day soon failed. And failure isn't pretty.
Whether it's lawn seepage, or backing up

into the basement, the tub, the washer,
or the toilet—wherever it can go.
And when they weren't wading

in their own waste, many
were scrambling to
buy ammunition.

I guess the news
wasn't shitty
enough.

Sin of Omission

I am best suited to silence.
What is left unsaid,
intentionally omitted
meant to be inferred.

I pride myself, in fact,
on being oblique.

But there is oblique,
and there is altogether absent.

Twice removed:
once from my source,
and now from myself.
I late received a passing mention,
if only as an exclusion.

Today it appears I am unworthy of that.

But I am more than a symbol of omission.
Intangible though it may be,
there is import to my being
and my uses.

My colleagues are but tools,
conveying form and context.
I am emotion,
tension,
nuance.

I am subtext.

Of course, these are not your concerns.

Your passion is for order.
And perhaps it is counter-intuitive to define
or impose structure
upon something whose very nature is
ethereal   intuitive

But what is the world without mystery?
And what is the written word
if it cannot conjure up that mystery,
if it spoon-feeds every idea
with precision and correctness?

What, in fact, is *style*, if everyone's is the same?

I am merely three dots.
Ignore them, and nothing terrible
or spectacular
will happen.

Connect them…
and you may touch the Elements.

New Year's Eve

No, my friend.
You were not just a thief,
slaughterer,
or scaremonger.

You may not have that satisfaction.

You took more than you gave,
but the sample you allowed
eclipsed the rest.

Despite the shockwaves
threatening past and future
and sucking the marrow from our joy,

your tangerine dreams,
your upside-down world and terrorist tactics,
served only to widen our eyes
and expand our hearts.

We have awoken from our sleep.
And you have simply strengthened
our purpose and resolve.

Tomorrow you will be a number
on a pair of plastic glasses,
while we take your measure

and rise above
to love each other once again.

The Spur

There's nothing "of the moment" about it.
Years in the making, like a barnacle,
it impales mobility and vanity with equal force.

Every poker-hot jab is a comment
on too-high heels, cockroach-killer toes,
and outgrown ski boots.

Contrary to its name, it offers no inducement
to move faster or try harder.
The only thing hastened is the demise of cartilage.

How cruel that when even hair has stopped growing
and bones are shrinking,
this volcano should erupt.

Elegy for an Irish Terrier

For Nell

A model of your standard you were not—
and though you had your charms, I must confess,
your breath was foul, your teeth were black with rot,
your oily skin discouraged a caress.

You lounged around, then slept all afternoon.
You wouldn't catch a ball and didn't swim.
The gas you passed could empty a saloon.
Your eyesight and intelligence were dim.

Perhaps your hair, a dirty shade of red,
accounted for some quirkiness and pluck,
You shredded Kleenex, stole and ate our bread,
and despite your Irish genes, had rotten luck.

This epitaph might come as a surprise:
You were the apple of your mistress's eyes.

Murmuration

The wanderers gaze in awe at the shape-shifting cloud
swirling and twisting into startling formations;
first an orb, now a leaping porpoise, a bow,
even a starling itself.

One morphing mass of individuals
feinting and diving in simultaneous waves
of life energy, the velocity of one affecting the whole
in scale-free correlation.

Every shift is a critical transition,
a synchronized orientation of
magnet shards, drawn together and apart,
electron particles spinning and aligning.

The observers murmur and gasp, enthralled by
the beauty and harmony of the display,
oblivious to the raptor
just outside the margins
or near the darkest center of the cloud
where individuals are packed the tightest.

PRISM

Schism

The crevasse
is deep and impenetrable,
its edges defined by sharp rock.

Its source,
once fed by glacial melt,
has long since dried up.

Wind-sheared trees
stand off on either side,
disfigured by the elements.

An eagle
riding the currents
across the divide

drops a seed
of hope.

Prism

No blue birds
only blue wavelengths
bouncing on particles
glistening blue

No blue eyes
only blue sky
dancing in fragments
sparkling blue

No blue sky
only blue light
surfing on air-streams
shimmering blue

No blue water
only blue cchoes
rippling the firmament
burnishing birds

Notes

"Joint Custody"
When I was researching the old TWA Flight Center at JFK
Airport for this poem, I was intrigued to discover that the
building had originally been called the "head house." Today it's
the TWA Hotel, but those memorable red passageways through
which I passed so many times as a child are still there, and still
evoke powerful sense memories of traveling back and forth
between my two families.

"Door to Door" and "Over the Tannoy"
My maternal great-grandfather, William Arthur Morris, was
a coal miner by day and a poet by night, earning him the moniker
"The Pitman's Poet." He made something of a name for himself
in the 1920s, performing his pieces at parties in and around
Swinton, in South Yorkshire, England, many of which celebrated
the "Pit Ponies" that worked underground in the mines.
Apparently, his poems were lucrative enough for some would-be
copyright infringers to attempt to steal them. Arthur eventually
contracted syphilis from his philandering, infected his wife, and
they both died in a sanitorium. In 2004, a local history buff from
Swinton by the name of Giles Brearley published a small
biography of Arthur's life that included some of his poetry. *The
Pitman's Poet: The Life and Times of Arthur Morris* served as
inspiration and source material for these two poems. A plaque
honoring Arthur is installed on the building where he lived—
located, ironically, in Temperance Street.

"Social Litany"
This poem is a response to Billy Collins's "Litany," which in itself is a response to (and borrows the first two lines of) an untitled poem by Belgian poet Jack Crickillon. Clearly, I have participated in too many online quizzes.

"Sonata"
Al Hirschfeld was an American caricaturist best known for his line-drawn portraits of celebrities, especially Broadway performers. After the birth of his daughter, Nina, he began hiding her name, written in capital letters, in his drawings. "NINA" would appear at least once and often numerous times in a sleeve, in hair (as it does in his portrait of Leonard Bernstein), or somewhere in the background. The number of NINAs concealed was shown by the number written to the right of his signature. Coincidentally, one of Bernstein's daughters—who happens to be a dear friend—is also named Nina.

"Lexington Avenue"
This "found poem" was the result of a walk down Lexington Avenue in New York City. The proliferation of signage assaulted my senses as much as the verbal catcalls.

"Homeland"
A gorgeous book entitled *Uncommon Ground: A Word Lover's Guide to the British Landscape* by Dominick Tyler, a documentary photographer, provided the inspiration for this poem, as well as for "Schism" on page 66. The book pairs Tyler's photographs of the many landscape features of Great Britain with the words used to describe them, most of which are as eclectic and poetic as the geographical curiosities themselves. Tyler's eloquent observations about the many types of British mud reminded me of Gerard Manley Hopkins's "Pied Beauty," whose structure I borrowed for this poem.

"Whodunit"
There was a strange period in 2012 when a series of pet alligators (at least seven) were abandoned in parking lots across Long Island. One was found in a plastic tub in the parking lot of an Applebee's Restaurant. Being a children's book author, I conjured an alliterative title for a picture book in the spirit of *Lyle, Lyle, Crocodile*... but the poem took me somewhere else entirely.

"Childishness"
A response to Frank O'Hara's "Autobiographia Literaria."

"High Hopes"
When our daughter Hope was born, a dear friend gave us a deciduous climbing rose, aptly called "High Hopes." It bears fragrant, double, light pink flowers.

"The Beauty of Anne Carson"
A response to Anne Carson's *The Beauty of the Husband: A Fictional Essay in 25 Tangos*.

The "Swamp Angel" poems
Prentice Mulford was a 19th century author and philosopher, born, raised, and buried in Sag Harbor, NY, where I live. These poems are inspired by his memoirs, in which he chronicles his time living off the grid in a cabin he built in a New Jersey swamp, while commuting daily to New York City to write news stories for *The New York Daily Graphic*.

I first came across Mulford when exploring our local cemetery in my teens. His epitaph reads: "Thoughts are things. - Mulford." I found this intriguing, and all the more so several years later when I discovered a small book entitled *Thought Forces*, penned by Mulford, on my mother's bookshelf. It was inscribed to her by my late great aunt, a converted Christian Scientist from England who adhered to Mulford's philosophies.

Mulford's father passed away when his son was just fourteen, leaving his child the sole proprietor of the Main Street hotel he owned and managed—a responsibility which proved too great, as the business went bankrupt four years later. Mulford spent the next four years in restless exploration, moving from job to job and generally acquiring the reputation of a "ne'er do-well." At twenty-two, he sailed for San Francisco during the last wave of the Gold Rush. He sought his fortune first in Jamestown, as a seagull egg sorter, cook, miner, schoolteacher, and lecturer, respectively. At one point he ran for mayor but lost because his speeches were "too flamboyant." When the local river flooded, destroying the entire summer's mining efforts, he penned a humorous essay for the newspaper and signed it "Dogberry," after the blustering police constable of Shakespeare's *Much Ado About Nothing*. "Dogberry's" work caught the eye of the editor of *The Golden Era*, a prominent literary journal, and Mulford was invited to join the staff. He soon became a fixture in San Francisco's literary circle, alongside Mark Twain, Bret Harte, and other members of the "Bohemian set."

Mulford remained uneasy in his skin, however, and in his early thirties, he converted to spiritualism. In the first of several attempts at a hermitic lifestyle, he bought an old whaleboat and spent the next few years living in San Francisco Bay, wearing only a weather-worn, knitted union suit. He continued to write, alternating between Dogberry's mischievous reportage and his own musings on mental and spiritual laws.

Mulford's friendship with Twain led him to London, where he was received as one of America's foremost writers—though he remained reluctant to accept the praise. There he met a girl named Josie Allen, whom he later married. When the couple returned to the States, he worked as a comic lecturer, poet, essayist, and news columnist. This latter job he found increasingly depressing, being "thoroughly saturated with the horrors consequent on civilization." His marriage foundered, apparently due to his relative disinterest in money. Josie resorted to nude modeling to augment their income, a fact which Mulford is said to have discovered by opening a pack of cigarettes inside which was his wife's portrait.

Returning to solitude, he built himself a one-room cabin in the swamps of Passaic, New Jersey, where he lived, Thoreau-like, for the next decade. It was there that he wrote his memoir, along with his life's work—thirty-six volumes on "spiritualistic and theosophic science," which were eventually serialized by his friend and publisher F.J. Needham as "*The White Cross Library.*"

At the age of fifty-seven, Mulford decided to return to Sag Harbor for good. His mother and sisters still lived there, and he had from time to time made visits to the island in a 16-foot dory which he called "White Cross." The little boat was kitted out with a stove, awning, bunk, and lockers for his provisions, writing utensils and banjo, and thus equipped Mulford set out for home. Less than a week later, the boat was discovered floating in Sheepshead Bay. Having suffered an apparent stroke, Prentice Mulford appeared to have died peacefully in his sleep, though alongside him were several letters written during the journey referring, among other things, to a desire to get "out of the world."

I remained fascinated by his story over the years, and at one point wrote an article about him for our local newspaper. I later discovered that a good friend lived for a time in Mulford's childhood home—where his mother and sister were still living when he died. My friend claims that her family often heard knocking sounds late at night, which they imagined to be Mulford's ghost still attempting to return home.

A poetry exercise based on a historical figure inspired me to take on Mulford's voice. I enjoyed it so much that I wrote seven poems, which comprise the "B" section of this book-length sonnet.

I still visit Prentice whenever I take a stroll through Oakland Cemetery.

"L.E.M."
I was six years old when the Apollo 11 Lunar Module landed on the moon. I remember watching the event with my family at the summer home of some close friends. It was hard to make sense of, given my lack of understanding of the events and the grainy picture on the black and white television set, but I knew something momentous was happening.

Twenty-one years later, my husband and I moved to Sag Harbor and converted an old industrial building on the wharf into a small professional theater. The building had a colorful past, having hosted a night club, and prior to that a roller disco, both of which I had attended in my youth. In the early 1900s, it had housed a torpedo factory, and in the 1960s it was a Grumman Aerospace plant where parts for the Lunar Excursion Module were built. Because the space was cavernous, empty, and painted black when we took it over, we joked that the lunar landing had actually been filmed there.

Twenty-five years later, I was working as writer and executive producer on a children's series for Netflix that was filmed at Grumman Studios in Bethpage, Long Island—which had previously been another Grumman plant. My office had a steel door at least six inches thick, upon which was a massive, bank vault-style lock. I was told that the room had been the overnight storage chamber for the L.E.M. while Grumman was preparing it for its launch. Apparently there was some concern that Russian spies might try to steal the engineering secrets, or even the module itself.

"Eruption"
I live in a resort community. In the midst of the COVID-19 pandemic, many second homeowners evacuated to their "safe haven" second homes, which were not designed nor intended for year-round living.

"Schism"
Inspired by the Alltchaorunn couloir in the Scottish Highlands, as described in Dominick Tyler's *Uncommon Ground*, and also by the 2020 election.

"Prism"
I was fascinated to discover that the color blue is rare in nature, and mostly manifests as a combination of light and reflection. Blue birds are not in fact blue, as they do not contain any blue pigment. The blue we see is a function of "light scattering," a reflection process akin to how a prism works. Similarly, blue eyes don't have any blue pigment, but get their color in the same way that the ocean and the sky do—by scattering light, so that more blue light is reflected back out. When we scoop water from the ocean into a bucket, we can see that it is actually colorless, and if we were to grind up a blue feather the resulting powder would be brown. I find this concept both magical and mystifying. It feels somehow connected to the making of art.

Acknowledgments

This collection of poems, written over the span of eight years, would not have been possible without the generous support of a great many people.

Robert Reeves and Carla Caglioti, Associate Provost and Assistant Dean of Stony Brook Southampton's MFA in Creative Writing and Literature, respectively, made it possible for me to pursue my Master of Fine Arts degree while simultaneously teaching for the same program. They bent over backwards to accommodate my schedule—forever complicated by other professional commitments—even when it meant my taking a temporary leave of absence from my studies and later resuming them. I am so very grateful for their advocacy on my behalf, and for their continued encouragement of my creative endeavors.

Many of these poems began their life in workshops. Among the brilliant faculty members with whom I was lucky enough to study are Billy Collins—who was kind enough to be the second reader for my thesis, Roger Rosenblatt, Jules Feiffer, Star Black, and Julie Sheehan, who ultimately became my thesis advisor. Julie's inspired teaching, quirky sense of humor, and unlimited support—not to mention her own artistry as a poet and her curiosity and compassion as a reader—were the foundation upon which my thesis was built. I own many favorite poetry collections, but the spiral-bound "Powers of Poetry" that Julie curated as reading material for one of her courses remains my most treasured.

Acknowledgments

The accommodation and encouragement of my administrative and faculty colleagues at Stony Brook Southampton—including Will Chandler, Peggy Grigonis, Frank Imperiale, Christian McLean, Susan Scarf Merrell, Kathy Russo, and Lou Ann Walker—helped to boost my confidence and made it possible for me to juggle so many professional, creative, and academic balls. I am also indebted to the many fellow MFA students who provided meaningful feedback on my work. If they found it awkward to be sitting alongside me in one class and taught by me in another, they were kind enough not to say so.

In this collection, I pay homage to many of the poets who have inspired me over the years. One to whom I owe special thanks is Marilyn Nelson. Marilyn's exquisite *Fortune's Bones: The Manumission Requiem* touched me so deeply that I was inspired to try my own hand at writing poetry in the voice of a historical figure. The "Swamp Angel" poems in Section III of this manuscript are the result. Imagine my honor when Marilyn graciously agreed to be the third reader for my thesis, and then went above and beyond the call of duty to provide comprehensive feedback and suggest line edits on every poem.

Heartfelt thanks to the Bridport Prize International Creative Writing Competition and their 2021 poetry judge Raymond Antrobus, who to my great astonishment awarded the first prize for poetry to my poem, "Over the Tannoy." I couldn't be more appreciative of that extraordinary honor—which I share with my great-grandfather, Arthur Morris, whose words comprise half the poem.

Other champions of this collection to whom I owe boundless thanks include my brilliant agent, Janine Kamouh, as well as Julie Colbert, Olivia Burgher, and Laura Bonner of William Morris Endeavor; my editor, Allison Adler, and the entire team at Andrews McMeel; and my longtime manager and friend, Steve Sauer.

Last but certainly not least, I acknowledge my family—my beloved husband, Steve, and our beautiful children, Sam and Hope, to whom this collection is dedicated. I know it wasn't easy having me so pre-occupied during the long pursuit of my MFA, and I am forever grateful for their understanding, encouragement, and support.

I also thank my parents, all four of whom are (or were) readers, writers, and poets in their own right... and who introduced me to the magic of the written word.

About the Author

EMMA WALTON HAMILTON is a *New York Times* best selling children's author, editor, stage and television writer and producer, and arts educator.

Together with her mother, Julie Andrews, she has co-authored over thirty books for children and adults, nine of which have been on the *New York Times* best-seller list. Emma's book for parents and caregivers, *Raising Bookworms: Getting Kids Reading for Pleasure and Empowerment*, premiered as a #1 best-seller on Amazon.com in the literacy category and won a Parent's Choice Gold Medal.

Emma was a two-time Emmy Award nominee for her role as Executive Producer and Writer for *Julie's Greenroom*, a children's television program about the arts created for Netflix, co-produced by the Jim Henson Company. Emma is also a Grammy Award–winning voice-over artist, having provided voicing for numerous audiobooks, including *Julie Andrews' Collection of Poems, Songs and Lullabies* (2010 Grammy Award, Best Spoken Word Album for Children), as well as for radio, television, theater, and industrial spots. Most recently, she served as the host of PBS's "An Evening with Lerner and Loewe - Broadway in Concert." She and her mother also co-host *Julie's Library*, a story-time podcast for families produced by American Public Media.

As a faculty member for Stony Brook University's MFA in Creative Writing and Literature, Emma teaches all forms of children's book writing and serves as Founder/Director of the Children's Lit Fellows program and the annual Children's Lit Conference, as well as Executive Director of the Young Artists and Writers Project (YAWP), an interdisciplinary writing program for middle and high school students. A former actress and theatre director, Emma was a co-founder of Bay Street Theatre in Sag Harbor, where she served as co-Artistic Director and Director of Education and Programming for Young Audiences for seventeen years.

Emma's poetry has been published in several print and online publications, including SCBWI's *Bulletin, Julie Andrews' Collection of Poems, Songs and Lullabies*, and *Treasury for All Seasons*, the Texas Education Agency's "State of Texas Assessment of Academic Readiness, Grade 5," and the 2021 *Bridport Prize Anthology*, where her poem "Over the Tannoy" was the first prize winner for poetry.

Door to Door

Andrews McMeel Publishing
a division of Andrews McMeel Universal
1130 Walnut Street, Kansas City, Missouri 64106

www.andrewsmcmeel.com

22 23 24 25 26 RR2 10 9 8 7 6 5 4 3 2 1

ISBN: 978-1-5248-7464-3

Library of Congress Control Number: 2022933809

Editor: Allison Adler
Art Director: Tiffany Meairs
Production Editor: Brianna Westervelt
Production Manager: Julie Skalla

Photography Credits
© littleny / Adobe Stock
© laurha / Adobe Stock
© piccaya / Adobe Stock
© ystewarthenderson / Adobe Stock
© vitaliy / Adobe Stock

ATTENTION: SCHOOLS AND BUSINESSES
Andrews McMeel books are available at quantity discounts with bulk
purchase for educational, business, or sales promotional use.
For information, please e-mail the Andrews McMeel Publishing
Special Sales Department: specialsales@amuniversal.com.